GREETINGS FROM
IOWA STATE FAIR
DES MOINES, IOWA

GREETINGS FROM IOWA STATE FAIR
DES MOINES, IOWA

GREETINGS FROM IOWA STATE FAIR
DES MOINES, IOWA

GREETINGS FROM IOWA STATE FAIR
DES MOINES, IOWA

GREETINGS FROM IOWA STATE FAIR
DES MOINES, IOWA

GREETINGS FROM
IOWA STATE FAIR
DES MOINES, IOWA

GREETINGS FROM IOWA STATE FAIR
DES MOINES, IOWA

GREETINGS FROM IOWA STATE FAIR
DES MOINES, IOWA

GREETINGS FROM
IOWA STATE FAIR
DES MOINES, IOWA

GREETINGS FROM
IOWA STATE
FAIR
DES MOINES, IOWA

GREETINGS FROM
IOWA STATE
FAIR
DES MOINES, IOWA

GREETINGS FROM IOWA STATE FAIR
DES MOINES, IOWA

GREETINGS FROM IOWA STATE FAIR
DES MOINES, IOWA

GREETINGS FROM IOWA STATE FAIR
DES MOINES, IOWA

GREETINGS FROM IOWA STATE FAIR
DES MOINES, IOWA

GREETINGS FROM
IOWA STATE FAIR
DES MOINES, IOWA

Printed in the USA
CPSIA information can be obtained
at www.ICGtesting.com
LVHW090354300524
781287LV00007B/742